ISBN 978-1-333-88186-3
PIBN 10740793

This book is a reproduction of an important historical work. Forgotten Books uses state-of-the-art technology to digitally reconstruct the work, preserving the original format whilst repairing imperfections present in the aged copy. In rare cases, an imperfection in the original, such as a blemish or missing page, may be replicated in our edition. We do, however, repair the vast majority of imperfections successfully; any imperfections that remain are intentionally left to preserve the state of such historical works.

English
Français
Deutsche
Italiano
Español
Português

www.forgottenbooks.com

Mythology Photography **Fiction**
Fishing Christianity **Art** Cooking
Essays Buddhism Freemasonry
Medicine **Biology** Music **Ancient
Egypt** Evolution Carpentry Physics
Dance Geology **Mathematics** Fitness
Shakespeare **Folklore** Yoga Marketing
Confidence Immortality Biographies
Poetry **Psychology** Witchcraft
Electronics Chemistry History **Law**
Accounting **Philosophy** Anthropology
Alchemy Drama Quantum Mechanics
Atheism Sexual Health **Ancient History**
Entrepreneurship Languages Sport
Paleontology Needlework Islam
Metaphysics Investment Archaeology
Parenting Statistics Criminology
Motivational

The Old Fairbanks House.

Abridged from a chapter in "Old Colonial Homes" written by Alvin Lincoln Jones, (1894.) Edited for this pamphlet by the Family Historian, (1908.)

IN some respects the homestead of the Fairbanks family is entitled to the first place in considering the claims of the numerous old houses in the State, to our regard and attention. It is, beyond comparison, more picturesque, and in its primitive simplicity it brings us nearer to a true understanding of the actual appearance and characteristics of the house of our forefathers, than any other house we have seen. It is true that some changes have been made : but these have been in the nature of repairs rather than alterations, and have merely served to keep the old house from falling to pieces. The shape, size, and finish appear to-day about the same as they have within the memory of the "oldest inhabitant."

From the outside it is difficult to realize that this is an occupied dwelling. It seems more like an ideal picture, brought before our wondering eyes by some magic power of art. The gray walls, tinted by the brush of Father Time with the natural stain of the rain-drops ; the moss grown shingles on the roof in varying shades of sage and mauve ; the brightness of the meadow carpet, stretching away to the south, dotted with the yellow white of the "Marguerite" and the butter cup ; the purple shadows on the tree-trunks and on weather-beaten clap boards — make a composition of form and color which is hard to equal. That the pictorial possibilities of the house and its surroundings are appreciated by students of art is apparent to any one who remains for any length of time at the house ; for hardly a day passes in the out-door season, that the grounds are not overrun by devotees of the easel and sketching-block, or the more numerous camera "fiends."

It is impossible, in one photograph, to show the construction of this house, much less its remarkable quaintness and picturesqueness. The most picturesque view is from the back, as it appears when approached from the railroad station. No other poiⁱt shows so well the lowness of the house as it nestles among the tall and stately trees. The colored frontispiece shows the front ; the house has apparently turned its back to the road, as if to court that retirement which is denied it. The eastern end is also very attractive, and is photographed more frequently than any other section of the house.

Facing southerly, the house stands on one of the best corner lots in the town. The large farm which once belonged to it has long since been divided and scattered among different branches of the family. The lot on which the house stands now, contains about one acre.

As we come to examine details, we shall see that the house is in three sections, a main part and two wings. The entire length of the house, including the wings is seventy-five feet. The main or middle part has a pitch roof extending down over the lean to at the back to within a few feet of the ground. Both wings are gambrel roofed. Long years ago, an Indian arrow projected from the roof, having been there beyond the memory of any of the family.

[It is a family tradition, that the arrow was shot in, during the Indian raids in the trying days of the past.]

As we stand before the front door we can count eight windows, of which no two are alike in size. Being irregularly placed as well, the effect is very peculiar. The boarding of the outside walk will also attract attention; for we may see an assortment of sizes, ranging from a narrow clapboard, four inches wide, to some heavy plank measuring twenty-one inches across. Contrary to the usual custom, we do not find the chimney and the front door exactly in the centre, one of the very few exceptions to this rule of building two centuries ago that we have seen. This deviation results in making one of the main rooms larger than the other. The old well, where formerly the well sweep hung, is front of the door, although the house is now supplied by the town water. [Through the kindness of one of the descendants a new well sweep has been placed in position.]

In addition to the main chimney we shall notice a smaller one in the eastern wing. The western wing never had a chimney, the rooms having been principally used by the hired men as sleeping apartments. Although connected with the main part by a door, it stands as a separate house, being built up against the older structure, as may be seen by an examination of the cellar. (This wing is supposed to have been built about 1654.)

The doorways throughout the house are so low that a person of medium height can scarcely pass through without bending the head. The lower front entry measures eight feet in depth. From this diminutive hall five doors open—the front outside door, those opening into the rooms on either side, a door at the foot of the stairway to the floor above, and another at the head of the stairs to the cellar. The back wall of the upper stairway is formed by the wall of the chimney, as is usual in houses of this period, and the bricks have never been covered. This is the only case of the kind we have ever seen. In the hall we first noticed the extent of the settling of the walk, the front wall having dropped little by little until the timbers which run from front to back have brokon clear through. Extra pieces have been put in as braces, some of them measuring eleven inches in length.

We passed into the kitchen at the left of the entry. Figuratively speaking, we passed from the end of the nineteenth century to the middle of the seventeenth century at the same time. No room in the house appears as old this kitchen. It is about sixteen feet square, and is only lighted by two long narrow windows on the front. Overhead all the beams and rafters show, this room never having been plastered. The walls are made of over-lapped boards with rounded edges. The outside walls were finished the same way before the clap-boards were put on. All the woodwork in the kitchen has turned to a deep brown, chocolate brown, the result of age and the smoke from the wood fires of two centuries. Years ago the overhead rafters were painted, but the paint now has almost entirely disappeared.

The old fireplace has been covered in, and a modern coal stove was used. The brick oven still remains, but has outlived its usefulness. The chimney at the bottom, measures eight by ten feet. [The covering of the fireplace has been removed (1908) and the original old crane found hanging in place.]

A door has been cut from the kitchen into the west wing, and another at the back leads to the room in the leanto. As the floor of the kitchen is a foot or more lower than the room in the leanto a square log has been placed in the doorway as a step. The smooth, deep hollow in the log, caused by the passing and repassing of the countless footsteps, was one of the most interesting features of the house. The baby, the child, the youth, the maiden, father, "grandpa" and "grandma" have left their imprint here. We missed the well-worn door-stone at the entrance but we found its substitute here.

Suspended from two hooks fastened into the great beam in the ceiling, we saw an old smooth-bore musket, two yards long. This gun has a famous history, having been carried to the siege of Louisburg by Lieut. Joseph Fairbanks. After the surrender, Joseph Fairbanks and his family settled at Halifax, where his descendants still remain. A few years ago the owner of the gun sent it to Miss Rebecca, and so the old smooth-bore came to be hung again in its old place after the absence of one hundred and thirty-five years. [This gun was sold by Miss Rebecca to Prof. Henry Fairbanks of St. Johnsbury, Vt., and is at present in the historic abode of that branch of the family.]

Crossing the entry we enter the parlor. This was originally about two-thirds the size of the kitchen. An addition was built on to the eastern end, adding about six feet to the width and allowing for two extra windows. The parlor has been plastered, and is in other ways more modern than the kitchen. It is one of the lowest in the house, measuring in the highest part not over six feet in height, and near the front wall which has sunk so much, it is several inches less. Here we found considerable old china and some very old books, and most valuable of all, a set of four colored pictures of the Lexington and Concord fight, by J. Honeywood. These are said to be the original drawings from which the reproductions which have appeared in some of the magazines were taken. One hundred and fifty dollars have been offered for them and refused.

The leanto contains a room back of the parlor, which was formerly a bedroom, and a long room back of the kitchen and chimney, once used as a sitting-room and work-room. The bedroom has one small window. The other room has two windows and an outside door, which, owing to the sinking of the walls, is now but four feet and four inches high.

Although the leanto is two steps higher than the main rooms, we must go up still another to enter the eastern wing. It is an old tradition in the family that this part was built for John Fairbanks and his bride in 1641, his father having erected the main structure five years before. With the exception of the kitchen we found this quite a cosy tenement, having two lower and one upper room. A very odd little porch has been squeezed into the corner of the house, opening from the larger room. A "settle" or seat fills up one side of the porch. This we are told, was a great place for "courting" in olden times.

The larger room in the wing was John's parlor. One window looks out beside the porch, and two others across the yard at the back. In the northeast corner is a chimney with a fireplace in each of the lower rooms. In the parlor, over the fire-place, still swings a wooden crane five feet long.

Long years ago, before the discovery of petroleum, the family used to hang grease lamps called "widders," or "old Bettsy," on this crane, to light up the room during the long winter evenings.

The tall old clock in the corner, although somewhat over 150 years old is a new comer to the house. It was bought from a family in New Hampshire a few years ago. For generations it had told the time in the same place; and the last owner received it as a legacy, with the condition that it should never be sold unless to provide food in case of great need. Years passed away and the struggle for food became more precarious, until finally the ancient heirloom was sold.

The small room in the wing was a chamber, and is only separated from the parlor by a board partition. The fire-place in the chamber was once ornamented with old fashionable blue Dutch tiles, two of which still remain. This room has two windows. [These two rooms have been repapered (1908) in dainty reproduction of an old style pattern.]

From the main room a winding stair ascends to the chamber above, which is as large as both of the lower rooms. These rooms in the wing are quite modern in appearance, being papered and painted; and seeming very comfortable. From the closet were brought for inspection two linen counterpanes of unknown age, woven in the house from flax grown upon the farm. Here too, we found a handsome linen table cloth

Original Parlor or Sitting Room

which belonged to Ebenezer Fairbanks junior, who lived on the old place from 1758 to 1832. It is probably over 100 years old, and the design represents the American Eagle and the motto "E Pluribus Unum." In the border is woven the name of the maker, W. W. Coulson, Lisburn, Ireland.

Retracing our steps, we found ourselves in the front entry again, from which we went up the enclosed stairway, where the chimney bricks show, to the floor above. The more we investigated this old part the more surprised we were that a wooden house could have stood so long with such slight changes. The great brown timbers show plainly here, the upright posts widening out at the top to support the transverse beams. Yet, despite the roughness of the finish, much care is apparent in the shaping and ornamentation of the timbers. It is the evidence of this nice carpentry which is relied upon as furnishing proof, that the timbers were brought from England, for which belief there is a well established family tradition. The upper entry is about the same size as the one below, and is lighted by one window, the outside size of the entire casement being 17 by 22 inches. The window-panes are 7 by 9 size.

The room over the parlor has been the family chamber through all the generations that have lived here. A great many of the best relics have been sold or given away, yet we find a store of curiosities remaining. A wooden tray, said to have been brought from

England, and a contribution box made of bark and fastened with thongs which was once passed around among the congregation at "clapboard trees" parish by Deacon Benjamin Fairbanks, were among the most interesting articles. [This contribution box sold by Miss Rebecca, has recently been returned to the family and is once more in the homestead.]

The kitchen chamber, like the room above, has never been lathed or plastered. It is a large room, yet the light is admitted by one small window, 20 inches high and 28 inches wide. The entire window swings outwardly from the side. Long we linger in this dark chamber, searching the dim corners for souvenirs of the days gone by. We found foot-warmers and spinning-wheels, candle moulds, Dutch ovens, and other articles of Domestic use. Then we ran across a pannier, such as our grandsires slung along the old mare's side when going to mill or up to the post office. An ox saddle was a still greater curiosity; yet from out of the depths of the gloom we brought to light the diamond-shaped panes still remaining. We had about given up all hope of ever finding any of these panes in any house in New England. They were brought from England, and set in strips of lead as putty was not in use at that time. The panes measured three and three-quarters inches across. The diamond-shaped pane was the first window-glass ever used in this country. The garret is reached by a ladder, and contains nothing but cobwebs. The eastern wing being newer, possessed no characteris cs differing from other houses we have vi 'ted.

So much for the hou :. What of its people? Shall we find th n as interesting f s the home they have li ?d in? Let us t ad and see.

There are persons still living who re- m mber Ebenezer Fairbanks, the last male of the line to live in the old homestead. He was a man of considerable importance in the town; a singer of more than local celebrity, his vocal gift securing him a po- sitiou in the choir of the Congregational Church as well as many invitations to join the " singin'-schools " of the neighboring towns.

He had eight children. Calvin the eld- est, died in 1800, at the age 22. His sec- ond son William, married Mille Farrington of Dedham, and had four children. The youngest Sarah was the wife of Augustus B. Endicott, sheriff of Norfolk County. William Fairbauks died Feb. 1, 1863, aged 78 years. Joshua, the youngest child of

Ebenezer was born Dec. 23, 1796. He lived at Dedham near the old homestead of which he inherited a part. He married Clarissa Bird of Stoughton in 1816 and had six children. The youngest was Rebecca who was the last owner of the ancestral home. Joshua Fairbanks died Oct. 27, 1865.

Of the five daughters of Ebenezer and Mary Fairbanks, two were married, — Sukey Davis Fairbanks to Jason Ellis of West Dedham, and Mary Fairbanks to Nahum Harrington of Westboro. (An an- cient map of our country, about one hun- dred years old, owned by Nahum and Mary has been returned (1907) to the house.)

The three unmarried daughters remained at home, and, after the death of their fa- ther, continued to occupy the old house till death separated them. Many stories have been told regarding the eccentricities of these three old ladies ; but, like all gossip, we found the most of the tales were not true. It was asserted that they could not agree together, and that each lived iu a separate part of the house, occupying individual chambers, and at times refusing to see each other for days and weeks at a time.

Indeed remorseless scandal mongers, regardless of probabilities, pointed at the three stair-cases, and asserted that these were built to accomodate the whims of these ill-assorted sisters. We want to state, as a matter of justice, that these things are not so. It is true that the sisters occupied separate appartments during the last years of their lives ; but it was not dislike to each other, but from the natural desire of old folks to be alone. They had their peculiarities, as might have been expected ; yet as long as they lived they had their meals together and attended to the household duties in turn, each one doing the work for a week. And although the dilapidation of the house made the task of keeping it in order rather dfficult, their housekeeping was of the first order. The painted stairs in the eastern wing, were never ascended without removing the shoes.

The woodwork was scrubbed and polished until it shone. We can well believe that the house was a pleasant home during the occupancy of the three sisters.

Prudence the eldest of the three, died March 26, 1871, at the ripe old age of 89 years, 11 months, and 12 days. Sarah or 'Sally' as she was called, died May 12, 1877, aged 87 years, 3 months, and 16 days. Nancy, the last of the family, died Jan. 19, 1879, aged 84 years, 4 months, and 16 days. Miss Rebecca Fairbanks lived at the old house with her three aunts during the last years of their lives.

Throughout the 258 years which have passed over it, the house has never been deeded. A Fairbanks built it, his descendants have always owned and occupied it. During the Summer of 1902 a severe thunderstorm passed over the town. Miss Rebecca was alone in the house and had just retired, her dog lying under the bed as usual. A bolt of lightning struck the house, passed through the room where Miss Fairbanks was lying and killed the dog.

Although much frightened, Miss Fairbanks was uninjured. Yet so strong was her dread of the place and of being alone there that she removed to Boston, the following winter. The house was let, and for the first time in its history it was occupied by strangers. Miss Fairbanks returned there the following summer, and remained until the estate was purchased by the "Fairbanks Family Association". The Fairbanks house proves a great attraction to visitors. At present it divides attention with the antiquarian society's rooms, at the centre of the town.

Jonathan Fayerbanke==His History.

By John Wilder Fairbank, Family Historian

TWO "Fairbanks" names appear on the early records of the Puritan Colony. Richard Fairebanke came to Boston in 1633, with his wife Elizabeth. It is thought that they came in the "Griffin," the ship which brought Rev. John Cotton to these shores. Savage, the historian says, that they united with the church a month after that great teacher's arrival, on the same day with Elder Leverett and his wife, Governor Brewster and Edward Hutchinson. It was "in ye 8th moneth, 1633," that these signed "ye covenant," and "in ye 9th moneth Elizabeth Fairebancke." Richard was prominently identified with the public affairs of the new settlement and held many town offices. He was a member of the Ancient and Honorable Artillery Company, and was the first Postmaster of the Colony. In 1639 the council granted the petition of the inhabitants and the following order was issued: "For preventing the miscarriage of letters, and it is ordered that notice be given Richard Fairebanke, his house in Boston is the place appointed for all letters which are brought beyond the seas, or are to be sent thither, are to be brought unto; and he is to take care that they be delivered and sent according to their directions; and he is allowed for every letter a penny, and must answer all miscarriages through his own neglect in this kind, provided that no man shall be compelled to bring his letter thither except he please." He probably served the people thus until his death, as we find nothing further said, until 1677, when the inhabitants of Boston again petitioned the council for a postmaster. We learn by deaths filed, that he died prior to April 15, 1667. He left no descendants in the male line, for as far as the records show, he had only two children, Zaccheus, the boy, dying at the early age of 14 years: Constance, the daughter, was born (bapt.) January 10, 1636, and married Samuel Mattock of Boston, March 30, 1653. Ten children were born to them, four only living to bring up families. The history of Richard Fairebanke is an interesting one, but our interest, as a family, is all centered in the other arrival.

Our Ancestor.

Jonathan Fayerbanke, is reported to have come from Sowerby, in the vicarage of Halifax, Yorkshire, England, to Boston, Mass., probably in 1633, at the same time that Richard came. It is not known for sure, but it is thought that they were brothers. The records on this side the water have been searched carefully, but thus far have failed to show the date of their arrival or their relationship. It is hoped that the searchings now going on in the mother land will determine these matters. With Jonathan, came his wife Grace and six children, John, George, Mary, Susan, Jonas and Jonathan. It is said that they brought with them the frame of a house , and that the timbers lay in Boston for three years, during which time Jonathan looked about for a location. He finally decided on Dedham, [Contentment as then called] where he settled in 1636. This old town, now quite famous, was established and named by the General Court on the "10th of ye 7th moneth 1636." (Sept. 10th) on the petition of twelve persons. Thereupon the "Dedham Covenant" was drawn up and signed by the petitioners and others. After the grant of the General Court in 1636, persons were admitted from time to time. On the 23d of March, 1637, "Jonathan Fairebanke" being presented by John Duite was accepted and subscribed.

The Covenant was in the nature of a mutual compact concerning the future management of the affairs of the town, and was as follows :

THE COVENANT.

1. We whose names ar here vnto subscribed, doe. in the feare and Reuerence of our Allmightie God, Mutually : and seuerally p'mise amongst our seules and each to other to p'ffesse and practice one truth according to that most p'fect rule. the foundacion where of is Eurlasting Love :

2. That we shall by all meanes Laboure to keepe of from vs all such as ar contrarye minded. And receaue onely such vnto vs as be such as may be p'bably of one harte, with vs as that we either knowe or may well and truely be informed to walke in a peaceable conuersation with all meakenes of spirit for edification of each other in the knowledg and faith of the Lord Iesus ; and the mutuall encouragmt vnto

all Temporall comforts in all things : seeke-
ing the good of each other out of all which
may be deriued true Peace.

3. That if at any time difference shall
arise betwene p'ties of our said Towne,
that then such p'tie and p'ties shall present-
ly Referre all such difference. vnto som
one. 2. or 3. others of our said societie to
be fully accorded and determined without
any further delay, if it possibly may be :

4. That every man that now or at any
time heere after shall haue Lotts in our
Towne shall pay his share in all such
Rates of money, and charges shall be
impored upon him Rateably in p portion
with other men As also become freely
subeject vuto all such orders and constitu-
tions as shall be necessariely had or made,
now or at any time heere after from this
daye fore warde, as well for Loveing and
comfortable societie, in ovr said Towne as
also for the p sperous and thriuing Condi-
cian of our said fellowshipe, especially
respecting the feare of Gód in which we
desire to begin and continue what so euer
we shall by his Loveing fauour take in hand.

5. And for the better manefestation of
our true resolution heere in. euery man so
receaud ; to subscribe heere vnto his name
there by obligeing both himgelf and his
successors after him for euer, as we have
done.

A Prominent Man.

We find that our ancestor was placed at
once on a special committee, that he was
present month by month at the meetings,
taking an active part in the affairs of the
town andthat he was a prominent man in
those early trying days. He was a man
with a good education for the times, a man
of strong common sense, sound judgement
and good executive ability.

"It seems evident," says an able cor-
respondent, "that he was a man of strong
individuality, and that characteristic, at

The Old Fairbanks House, Dedham, Mass.   (South Front)
Built 1636-48-54

least, his descendants undoubtedly retain to a large extent, for we find many instances of dogged tenacity of purpose marking the actions of individuals in each generation, by means of which they have raised themselves to high rank in their respective callings, and we are fully entitled to claim that the average position which has been attained by the menbers of the family in the communities in which they have labored, has been such as to mark it as a family second to none in any respect on this side of the Atlantic."

He was evidently possessed of ample means for those days, or he would not have been able to have taken good care of his large family until he secured his permanent home. He received various grants of land in Dedham at different times, including the lot on which the house now stands. Before 1637 there had been granted him a twelve acre lot, four acres of which were "Swampe" land; and in that year he received another allotment of four acres more.

In those early days lands were granted to individuals in twelve and eight acre lots, the grants reading thus:

"Ordered that euery Twelve Acre Lott shall have foure acres of swampe granted in the first graute there vnto besides what may be granted in any deuident of swampe that may afterwards be layed out."

Another order read:

"Ordered that euery man that hath an whole Lott shall haue so many Acres of Meadowe as he hath vpland in his first grante for a house Lott where of part of such pcells of meadowe as lyeth adioyneing to his said Lott shall be granted to him in pt and the remainder shall be made vp else where."

In 1642 he was granted "Sixe acres in ye medowe neere vuto the south side of Ballpate hill." Two other grants appear on the recods in 1644, and in 1656 he was alloted his proportion of "Comon town rights," six and three-fourths acres.

The Ancestral Home.

On tne "vpland in his grant for an house Lott," made in 1636, our ancestor built his first house, or rather a part of the present building, in which they lived subsequently; about 1648, an addition was built, and a few years later, a larger addition was made, which was called "the new house," supposed to be built for the occupation of his oldest son John and his family. There the historic old house has stood till the present· time, "warped .and worn by the sunshine and storms" of nearly three centuries. "Winter and summer, frost and heat have done much to undermine its symmetry, and its leaning walls and sloping floors are only held in.place by its massive oak." During all this time down to 1897, it has been handed down through eight generations with never a mortgage incumbrance upon it.

As to Jonathan's "gude wife," we know nothing at present, but we can not but feel that she was "a fair woman to look upon" and that there was no holding back, when the call came to her husband as it did to Abram of old, "Get thee out of thy country, and from thy kindred, and from thy father's house unto a land that I will show thee, and I will make of thee a great nation, and I will bless thee and make thy name great, and thou shalt be a blessing." It is only recently (1903) that her name and date of marriage have been discovered, all of the Dedham records simply saying, "Jonathan and Grace." Probably at some future time, we may learn of her parentage as well as that of Jonathan the husband, as researches are now being carried forward in the country about the old Sowerby hamlet. The Halifax parish register (a few miles from Sowerby) has this record : "1617, 20 May Nup. Jonathan Fayrbanke—? and Grace Smith War." War stands for Warley, probably the home of Grace. The same parish register has this record : "Sowerby, George Fayerbanke. Church warden." He was a cousin (of some degree) of Jonathan as the following testifics : *

This handsomely written copy was folded and sealed, like a letter, without envelope, and addressed in a different handwriting from the copyist's

George ffairebanke his
   last Will &
   Testamt.
      ffor his Lovinge Cousen Jonathan
      Fayrebancke in new Ingland
      these
         Delivr.

The last Will and Testament of George ffairbanke of Sowerby in ye Vickeridge of Halifax & County of Yorke, Clothier
      May ye xxviijth. 1650

Conserninge ye Disposal of all my world-ly goods : ffirst my will and minde is yt all my lawfull debts ffuneral expenses & charges I haue putt Iames Platts to in this my sickness bee paid out of my whole Estate ; And then my will & minde is as followeth :

Jnprimis J giue and bequeath to Mr. Henery Roote fforty shillingr ; J giuc & bequeath to ye poore of Sowerby ye Sum'e of xls to be distributed amongst them as my Executor shall thinke most fitt ; J giue & bequaith to Michael ffairebanke my brother xls.; J giue & bequaith to my brother Deanes' Children wch hee had by my Sister xls. ; J giue & bequaith to my brother John Axenoppe xls. ; J giue and bequaith to Ellis Rutters & his wife xls. ; J. giue and bequaith to my brother Jeremias wife and Children xxxs. equally to bee deuided amongst them ; J giue and be-quaith unto ye Children of Henery Blackley hee had by my sister Abigall xxs. ; J. giue & bequaith to Mr. Jonathan ffairbanke xxs; J. giue & bequeath to Sushan Chad-wicke ffieu pounds; J giue & bequeath to George ffairebanke sonne of George ffaire-banke ye sum'e of 5£ ; J guie & bequeath to Abraham Platts pe sum'e of 6£ ; J giue & bequeath to Nathan Bates sonne of Mathew Bates xs ; J glue to Henery Stanhops xijd ; J giue to Nathan Hobroyd ijs vjd ; J giue to Sara Chadwicke daughter of Sushan Chadwiche vs ; J giue to Nicholas Cunliffe 5s ; J giue to Grace Kiluer xs ; J giue to Nathan Carter sonne of Michaell Carter deceased ffive shill. ; J giuve to Sara Platts ffive shill. ; J giue to James Sharpe ffive shill.; J giue to James Casson xs ; J giue & bequeath to Mary Platts wife of James Platts wth whome J now live 5£ J give & bequethe to Sarah Platts daughter of James Platts 3£ I giue to Iohn Bawden & his wife xs ; I giue to Mary Earneshawe and her three Children, eury one of them xs ; J giue to Michaell Earneshaw, my Purple suite, one ffustion doublett with silver buttons at ; J giue & bequeath to James Platts with whom I now lieu x£ as also a newe peece of cloath Tanney C[ou]ller to be him a suit ; & all such things as to make vpp complete for weareinge, J giue & bequethe to Samuel ffarrer ye summe of 5£ pvided hee bee Lieueinge twelue mouthes after my death.   Alwayes pvided & my will

& minde is yt my Executer shall not paye Legacyes till ye suites now commenced against any pson or psons bee fully ended & if it so fall out yt ye suite or suits commenced doe call for & expend more then is expected so yt theire is not sufficient to paye ye legacyes giuen then my will & minde is yt eury one shall baite of his Legacie accordinge as my Estate shall fall short ye residue of my goods Cattles & Chattles vndiposed of J giue and bequeth to James Platts whom J ordaine and appointe sole Executer of this my last will and Tetament & I doe hereby revoke all other wills whatsour.   In Witnes whereof I haue putte my hand.   In ye presence of witnesses Robert Tilletson Mary Platts Grace Lee Abraham Platts.

Vera Copia   Concordance with original.

This is an interesting document both as to loving remembrance and showing the relationship existing between George and Jonathan, also that the famous John Prescott, the founder of Lancaster, Mass., whose daughter Lydia married Jonas, the third son of Johnathan, was also "in the family," as his wife was Mary Platts.

Of the children of Jonathan and Grace we have not space to say much about them in this article. At some subsequent time we will relate their "going outs." They were all strong characters, well fitted to be the "fathers of towns," as they at least were. Following the English law of entail, John, the oldest son, came into possession of the homestead and from that time down to 1897, the old house was continuously occupied by him and his descendants, through eight generations, to Rebecca the last of the family tenants. The following document is of much interest:

* Latest information (1908) seems to point to his being a younger half brother of Jonathan.

WILL OF JONATHAN FARABNKE OF DEDHAM

1668

In the yeare of our Lord one thousand sixe hundred sixty and eight, the first day of the fourth month, com'only called June, I Jonathan ffarbanke of dedham in the Countie of Suffolke Senioe, Being sicke and weake, And expecting that my day of desolution is drawing neere doe in the name and feare of God ordaine and make this my last will & Testamt for the disposeing and settling of the things of this life, with which the Lord hath at present Intrusted me in manner & forme as followeth ; viz ffrst I commit my soule to God that gaue it, Trusting in the alone Righteousnes & mediation of Jesus Christ my Redeemer and aduocate, & my body to the earth whence it way taken : to be after my decease, Desently buried therein in christin buriall at the discretion of my Executor. In prims I giue and bequeath vnto grace my Deere & well beloved wife, All and Every prt and prcell of my all moueable Estate whatsoeuer as well within doors as without, namely all my household sruffe, of all & Euery sort & kinde as also all my cattell of all kinds all my corne cartes ploughs workeing tooles & vtensils of husbandrye all debts due to me & whatsoeuer Ells come within the denomination of moueable Estate & all this I giue and Bequeath to my said wife, to despose as when And to whom shee shall at any time see meete. And more I giue to grace my said wife an Annuitie of Eight pound pr Annm to be paid to her or her assignee to her vse yearely and euery yeare, in two equall parts.** Ite I giue & bequeathe to George (ffarbanke my secon)d sonne & to his heyres for euer, sixteene pounds the one halfe weereof shall be payed to him within the space of one (- - - -) yeare next ensueing after the decease of my wife; And whereas I have allready giuen and doe hereby confirme to my said sonne George all that my prt in the general deuident (dividend?) already laid out thro Meadfield & some working tooles & such like small things, my will & my mind is, That the said parcell of lande and those tooles and other small things soe giuen shall be all indifferently and Equally aprized and if they shall together amount to the value of eight pounds then it shall be accounted for his first payment. *** And I giue and bequeathe to my daughter Mary the wife of Christofore Smith the summe of sixteen £ I giue to my said daughter in prticuler, & distinct from her husbans Estate & to be allwayes at her dispose, this sixteen pounds to be payed in two equall (sum'es?) of Eight pounds.*** Item More I giue to my said daughter Mary Three pounds to purchase her a suite of apparell to be paid within the space of three months after my decease. Item I giue and bequeath to Jonas ffarbank my third sonne & his heyres for euer like the sume of sixtene pounds to be allso payed in two equal sumes.*** I giue and bequeath to Jonathan ffarbanke

payment whereof is not named shall be al^l
payed in current Contrey payment at price
then Currant In ded[ham I guie & baque-
ath] To John ffarebanke my Eldest sonne
all my houses & lands whatsouer, not being formerly aboue [mentioned ? togeth]er
with all my common Rightes & towne pru-
iliges whatsoeur, to haue posses & enjoy
the same (– – –) & his heyers (– – – to)
enter vpon all my lands forthwith after my
decease ; and all my houses and yardes at
the end of foure mo'nthes n(ext followin)g
the same ; Item I do nominate apoint and
ordayne John Fairebancke my afforsaid
Eldest Sonne, To be my sole Executer to
whom I commit all necessary trust & power
Requisete for the due and full prformeance
& Execution of this my last will as it be-
longs or is necessary for an Executor to
doe in all & eury prt as is aboue expressed ;
Item I allso name & entreate my very lou-
i:ng friends Eleazer Lusher & Petter Wod-
ward Seue to be ouerseesr to the perform-
once of this my present will & to be

assisting to my aboue named Execuctor therin as themselves shall see cause, & I do hereby reuoke & make null & voide all others or former wills whatsouer by me formerly made ; & doe avouch & decleare this present writing, as is aboue herin entered. to be & contayne my true onely & last will & testemant.

In witnes whereof I the said Jonathan ffarebanke Sene haue herevnto subscriced my hand & affixed my seale the day & yeare first aboue written.

This is a true copy of the will of Jonathan Fayerbanke senyore.

as attest Daniell ffisher.

William Avery.

The inventory of the estate is interesting as showing the valuation of property and something of the habits of life at that time. The whole amounted to 214 pounds 04s 02d. which was quite a large estate for those early days.

INVENTORY OF THE ESTATE OF JONATHAN FAIRBANKE.

An Jnventory of the whole Estate of Jonathan Fairbanke Sene late of Dedham deceased made and taken ye 16th of 10th mo. Anno 1668 by those names are underwritten.   Viz.

Jn the parlenr
  Jn pmis ye bookes   00-18-00
  Jn money 9s 8d the purse in
    which the money was 4d   00-10-00
  Jte the weareing woolen Apa-
    rill of the deceased, with
    one hatt, with boots & cet.   05-07-00
  Jte weareing linen   01-01-00
  Jte bedstead matt and bed-
    coarde   00-10-00
  Jte 4 bed Curtaynes   00-15-00
  Jte one blew Rugg 2 blankets
    and one payer of sheets   03-15-00
  Jte 1 slack bed one Fether
    bolster 2 fether pillwes &
    2 pillow beers   02-00-00

Original Old Kitchen. (The same in 1908 as in 1636)

Jte one trundel beadstead bed
coarde and matts 00-06-00
Ite one toilet—one blanket
1£—one bedteak 5s 01-05-00
ite 2 feather pillowes 00-12-00
Jte one Livery Cupboarde, 01-05-00
Jte one sea (tea?) chest 00-03-00
Jte 2 Cleve,s, 00-06-00
Jte one olde Warmeing panne 00-02-06
Jte one Sunne Dyall 2s one
dryeing iron Is one door 00-04-00
Jte one Sworde 8s one Cuwte-
las 4s 00-12-00
Jte 2 gunnes 1 pound one musket
rest 1s 01-01-00
Jte one half pike 2s 6d one
gragno staffe 1s one other
small staffe 4 00-03-10
and other items
Jn the Halle (kitchen)
Ite 2 old Tables and one
forme 3-6d one Cbeyer 2-6 00-06-00
Ite one brasse Skillet 5 one
other olde skillet 1s 6d 00-06-06

Ite one olde kettle 7s one
Jron pot 5s 2pr pott hooks
2s-6 00-14-06
Ite 2Bakers 2-6 2Cokrows
10s fire shovell & tongs 5s 00-17-06
Ite Pewte(?) 2s one fryeing
panne 2s 00-04-00
Jte 16 wooden platters 1s 6d
one boxe 9 00-02-00
Ite 2 wooden bottles 1s one
tobacco knife and trencher
8d 00-01-08
Ite 6 aloamin spoones 1s 3d
one pewter wine (?) cupp 3d 00-02-00
Ite 4 pewter Dishes 8s 2 pieces
of old pewter 1s 00-09-00
Ite one painted Dish one gully
dish 1s 00-01-00
Ite 4 spinning wheeles 00-02-00
and other items
In the parlour Chamber
Ite one bedstead line & mat
8s th bedding hereupon
2 pounds 8s 02-16-00

Ite one piece of new cotton
  cloath,   00-18-00
Its 3 sheets 2 pillow beers one
  short table cloath   03-00-00
Its 12 pieces of linnen 14s 2
  old sheets 3 pieces of old
  linnen 5s. new linnen 15 yds.
  2-1.11   02-10-00
Jte one piece of english cotton
  on (one) snap sash— one
  poulder horne & poulder in it 00-05-00
Jte one Chest and one(.....)   00-07-00
In the rooms called the new
  house, *and* in the chamber
  of the new house, *many
  items farming*, *tools* corn rye
  peas wheat hemp and flax
In the working cellar
  Item 2 vices and one turning
  laeth and other Seueh things
  belonging to that roome   01-00-00
In another cellar
  Ite 4 beere possets one Churne,
  cheese, butter, beefe, &c.,   01-17-00

In the cellar in the yarde
  Ite 4 barreles with Cider in
    them one pouldering*(pow
    dering salting)* tubb wth
    some pork in it—and apples   01-16-00
In the hafe chamber
  Ite many Smale tools for turn-
    ing and other the like work, 03-00 00
  Jte sheeps wool and cotton
    woole 8s linnen yarne and
    cotton yarne 12s 3 tubbs
    one keeler one screw & c   01-00-00
  Ite scales and weights—and
    lead 4s6d   00-04-06
    hopps in a bag   00-01-06
In the purvis
  Jte Some Indian and one old
    fanne   00-04-00
In the yarde
  Jte one Cider presse with the
    things belonging thereto
    and g.ined estones   01-00-00
Jn cattell
  Jte 3 swine 2pounds5s with the
    piggs belonging thereto   02-05-90

4 Cowes and one yearning
Calf   14-00-00
2 Steeres about 4 yeares old   08-00-00
Jte haye in the barn and bar
  floores   03-00-00
Jte the home Lott with the
  adition of Lande in the
  wigwam playne—the orch
  yard and all the buildings
  thereupon   50-00-00
Jte the 8 Cows Comons   16-00-00
Jte 6 acres of meadowe in
  Broade meadowe   5-00-00
Jte 2 acres at forest meadow
  and Comon meadow shore   6-00-00

Jte in purgatory playne—22
  acres uplands   22-00-00
Jte in the Lowe playne - -
  acres   8-00-00
Jte North Deuideus 4 acres   12-00-00
Jte in the Clapboarde trees 02-00-00
Jte Swampe in the great
  Ceader Swampe neer sawe
  mille   1-00-00
Jte at moolomonupongo 3 Cow
  Comous   08-00-00
Jte rights at Porrosum Pranlo 03-00-00
      Elza Lusher
      Petr Woodward See
      Daniall ffisher

The Family Record

The first family record reads thus :
  Jonathan Fayerbanke was born in England, probably about 1595. He married,
(Halifax, England, parish register) May
20, 1617, Grace Smith of Warley, England.

He died in Dedham, Mass., December 5,
1668 ; she died either December 28, 1673,
or May 19, 1676.
  Their children were all born in England.
  1. John, born (bapt) February 15,

1617-18; married, March 1, 1641, Sarah Fiske. They lived on the Dedham homestead, where he died November 13, 1684; she died Nov. 26, 1683. Five children.

2. George, born (bapt) November 28, 1619; married, October 26, 1646, Mary Adams of Dedham. They removed to Sherborne, afterwards Medway, where he was an esteemed citizen. He was drowned January 10, 1682. His wife died August 11, 1711. Seven children.

3. Mary, born (bapt) Feb. 3, 1621-2; married, April 2, 1644, Michael Metcalf, Jr., who was born in England, August 29, 1620. He died March 1, 1654, and she married secondly, August 6, 1654, Christopher Smith of Dedham. She died June 4, 1684. He died November 7, 1676. Five children by first husband, one by the latter.

4. Jonas, born (bapt) March 6, 1624-5; removed to Lancaster, Mass., in 1657, where he married, May 28, 1658, Lydia, daughter of the famous John Prescott who also came from Sowerby, England. He was killed by the Indians, February 10, 1676, during a raid upon the settlement. Seven children.

5. Susan, born (bapt) Dec. 10, 1627 at Thorne; married, October 12, 1647, Ralph Day of Dedham. She died July 8, 1659. Six children.

6. Jonathan, born about 1628-9; resided in Dedham near his brother John. He married Deborah, daughter of Edward Shepard of Cambridge. He died Jan, 28, 1711-12; she died September 7, 1705.

Nearly all persons in the United States bearing the name of Fairbank or Fairbanks, are related by direct descent from Jonathan the first, while there are many others who take a pride in tracing their lineage back through the daughters to the original family tree.

Michael Metcalf Family.

MICHAEL Metcalf, the emigrant ancestor of this family, was born in Tatterford, County of Norfolk, England, baptized "17th die June 1587." He married Sarah, daughter of Thomas and Elizabeth Ellwyn, Oct. 13, 1616. She was born in Heigham England, on the 17th of June, 1593.

His father Leonard Metcalf, narrowly escaped the scaffold in 1569, when he joined in the rising in the North, in the interest of Mary, Queen of Scots. He was captured and condemned, but his execution was "stayed" to wait the Queen's pleasure,—and finally he was released, as he was announced to be "a very quiet honest gentleman" His large estates at Yorkshire, however, were taken from him, after which he left the country and settled in Norfolk, where several of his children were born. It was in troublous times that Michael was born ; being a very zealous nonconformist, he was often involved in controversies with his Bishop. By occupation he was a "Dornix weaver." This Dornix was a kind of stuff used for Curtains, Carpets and Hangings. So called from Doornick or Tournay, a city in Flanders, where it was first made. He was highly thought of, a prominent man in the city of Norwich, where he was made a freeman, June 21, 1618. Eleven children were there born to Michael and Sarah. Being a zealous Puritan he was hated and bitterly persecuted by the Bishop of Norwich, Matthew Wren, who twenty years afterwards, when Cromwell was in power, was brought to trial for his persecution of the Puritans. The days came when Michael was obliged to flee for his life, and the following extracts are taken from a copy of his letter written in Plymouth, England, Jan. 13, 1636, directed, "To all the true professors of Christ's Gospel within the City of Norwich."

"I was persecuted," he writes, "in the land of my fathers' sepulchres, for not bowing at the name of Jesus, and observing other ceremonies in religion forced upon me, at the instance of Bishop Wren of Norwich, and his Chancellor Dr. Corbet, whose violent measures troubled me in the Bishop's Court, and returned me into the High Commisioner's Court. Suffering many times for the cause of religion, I was forced, for the sake of the liberty of my conscience, to flee from my wife and children, to go into New England; taking ship for the voyoge at London the 17th of Sept. 1636; being by tempests tossed up and down the seas till the Christmas following; then veering about to Plymouth in Old England, in which time I met with many sore afflictions. Leaving the ship I went down to Yarmouth, in Norfolk County, whence I shipped myself and family to come to New England; sailed 15th April, 1637 and arrived three days before mid-summer, with my wife, nine children and a servant." In a postscript he remarks, "My enemies conspired against me to take away my life, and sometimes, to avoid their hands, my wife did hide me in the roof of the house, covering me with straw."

This letter from which the extracts are taken, is a long one, written probably after his first attempt to leave; he speaks of himself as an *exile* from his wife and children, "with whom he would gladly have continued, *if with liberty.*" This letter will be printed in full with others in the 'Metcalf Geneology; data for which is gradually being secured by the Family Historian.

He settled at once in Dedham near to his old friend Jonathan Fayerbanke, where he was admitted a townsman, July 14, 1637, joining the church in 1639, made a selectman in 1641. His name stands first in the committee chosen to "contrie the fabricke of a meeting house."

Here his eldest son Michael, met and won his bride, Mary, the eldest daughter of Jonathan Fayerbanke. To them five children were born. Michael Junior died in the 34th year of his life; Mary afterwards married Christopher Smith of Dedham, by whom she had one son.

The descendants of Michael and Mary are now numbered by the many thousands, composing names eminent in Literature, Science, Politics and Art—such names as the Ware's, Everett's, Huntington's Quincys'.

CPSIA information can be obtained
at www.ICGtesting.com
Printed in the USA
BVHW05s1341030818
523477BV00021B/873/P

9 781333 881863